# IH8U

1
c
abuse

S02018T-Black

## WAN2HELP?

We are constantly updating our files of text messages and emoticons for the next edition of this and our other text message books. If you would like to add variations of your own please e-mail us at

jokes@michaelomarabooks.com

We will let you know if your additions are going to be included. Thank you

# IH8U

ltle bk

of txt

abuse

First published in Great Britain in 2001 by
Michael O'Mara Books Limited
9 Lion Yard
Tremadoc Road
London SW4 7NQ

A CIP catalogue record for this book is available from the British
Library
ISBN 1-85479-832-4

1 3 5 7 9 10 8 6 4 2

Devised by Jamie Buchan
Compiled and edited by Gabrielle Mander

Cover Design: Design 23
Telephone supplied and used by kind permission of Motorola.

Designed and typeset by Design 23

www.mombooks.com

Made and printed in Great Britain by William Clowes, Beccles, Suffolk

# CONTENTS

# IH8U

Oh really? Of course not, but using your mobile phone or e-mail can be a great way to send light-hearted insults to friends who share your sense of humour, and sometimes talking turkey is the only way to get rid of those pests who just won't take 'No' for an answer.

**IH8U** has over 1000 abbreviations, acronyms and emoticons to choose from, so you will be sure to find a put-down, a sharp remark or a bare-faced insult for every occasion.

All mobile phones vary, but access to the messaging service is usually simple. Go to '**Menu**' and scroll to '**Messages**' then to '**Message Editor**'. Compose your message by using the letter and number keys on your phone. Each key represents more than one letter and symbol in both upper and lower case so you need to press repeatedly until the letter you want appears. Press the # key to stop the letter flashing. When your message is complete press '**ok**' and your message will be sent.

A few hints might be useful. The fewer characters without spaces between words, the speedier and less expensive your message will be.

Start each new word with a capital letter. A capital can also mean a long sound. A capital in the middle of a word can also mean a double letter: so **BAB = Baby** and **BuBle = Bubble**. A **$** sign means double S thus **SC$ = Success**. A full list of the basic shortcuts and abbreviations is given in **Bak2YaROts.**

Remember though, you can never have too many friends, so don't send insults that will really hurt and don't send obscenities.
That being said, gloves off, make e-nemies and **NMMr/MsNG** with **IH8U**.

# SASMBMBBNCNHM

**Sticks and stones...acronyms and abbreviations**

| | |
|---|---|
| **BLNDE** | blonde |
| **BItMe** | bite me |
| **EMS** | eat my shorts |
| **FMDIDGAD** | frankly my dear, I don't give a damn |
| **FOAD** | go away please |
| **GTASW** | goodbye, that's all she wrote |

| | |
|---|---|
| **HHIS** | hanging head in shame (not) |
| **H8** | hate |
| **IH8U** | I hate you |
| **ITYFIR** | I think you'll find I'm right |
| **IUTLUVUBIAON** | |
| | I used to love you but it's all over now |
| **KMA$** | kiss my ass |
| **KMB** | kiss my butt |

| | |
|---|---|
| **LAB&TUD** | life's a bitch and then you die |
| **LOMBARD** | loads of money but a right dickhead |
| **MMDP** | make my day punk! |
| **MOB** | mother of blonde |
| **MYOB** | mind your own business |
| **PDK** | polyester double knit |
| **PDS** | please don't shoot |
| **PITA** | pain in the ass |

**PITB**      pain in the butt

**PITN**      pain in the neck

**ROTFL**     rolling on the floor
              laughing

**ROTFLUTS**  rolling on the floor
              unable to speak

**ROTFLWTIMiis** rolling on the floor with
              tears in my eyes

**RSN**       really soon now

**SASMBMBBNCNHM**
              sticks and stones may
              break my bones, but
              names can never hurt me

| | |
|---|---|
| **SHID** | slaps head in disgust |
| **SOHF** | sense of humour failure |
| **SOS8N** | spawn of satan |
| **SSM** | so sue me |
| **TIC** | tongue in cheek |
| **TIOLI** | take it or leave it |
| **UTLKIN2ME?** | you talking to me? |
| **WTH** | what/who the heck |
| **WUCIWUG** | what you see is what you get |

| | |
|---|---|
| **YBS** | you'll be sorry |
| **YYSSW** | yeah, yeah, sure, sure, whatever |
| **\*G\*** | giggle or grin |
| **\*S\*** | sob |
| **+!** | yes |
| **-!** | no |
| **+!!** | very much so |
| **-!!** | definitely not |

# LtMeDrawUAPctur
**Let me draw you a picture – emoticons**

| | |
|---|---|
| **:@))** | you are a double-chinned fat pig |
| **U*8=(:** | you blithering idiot |
| **:-)** | ha ha |
| **{}** | no comment |
| **%+{** | you are a loser |
| **:*(@)** | you are drunk and shouting |

| | |
|---|---|
| (:-D | blabber mouth |
| I-O | I am bored |
| 4/> <: -}) | you are behaving like an estate agent |
| §;-( | you are behaving like a lawyer |
| :-o zz z z Z  Z | I am bored, bored, bored |
| :^U | I turn my face away |
| :-P | nyahhhh! |
| <=\ | I am slightly offended |

| | |
|---|---|
| **l : )** | monobrow (missing link) |
| **:-C** | I am really bummed |
| **o'P** | I stick my tongue out at you (profile) |
| **o'r** | sticking tongue out (profile) |
| **:-t** | it's no good looking cross and pouting |
| **%-<l>** | I am drunk with laughter (not) |
| **:-W** | liar (forked tongue) |

| | |
|---|---|
| (><) | you are anally retentive |
| :+( | I am hurt by that remark |
| :~( | I'm feeling put out |
| )I-[ | you are tired, grumpy and very sad |
| B-D | serves you right, dummy!! |
| >w | oh really! (ironic) |
| (O—< | fishface |
| -/- | you are a stirrer |

| | |
|---|---|
| @*&$!% | you know what that means... |
| >;-(' | er! dumb or what? |
| O-G-< | me, me, me, that's all you ever think about |
| <:-( | dunce |
| :-)= | goofy |
| <) | drip |
| <:-/ | pointy head |
| :-¥ | shut up! |

| | |
|---|---|
| : (:) | you pig! |
| :8) | pig yourself |
| 3:-o | silly moo |
| ::-( | four eyes |
| :-§( | call that a moustache? |
| :-))) | how many chins is it now? |
| :-)— | 98-pound weakling |
| !-( | I'd like to thank whoever gave you that black eye |

| | |
|---|---|
| **(-)** | get your hair cut |
| **:-D** | yes I am laughing at you |
| **\*!#\*!^\*&:-)?** | schizophrenic? I don't like either of you |
| **\*:o)** | bozo |
| **>:)** | little devil |
| **C:-)** | large brain – no ideas |
| **{(:-)** | no one loves a man with a bad toupee |
| **]:->** | Satan's spawn |

| | |
|---|---|
| **8:]** | gorilla |
| **:-%** | merchant banker |
| **:-F** | you are a bucktoothed vampire with one tooth missing, so bite me |
| **:-)'** | shall I get you a bib? |
| **:-@** | did you ever model for Picasso? |
| **:-I** | have an ordinary day |
| **%-)** | cross-eyed |

| | |
|---|---|
| Ø;^) | do you come from another planet? |
| =^..^= | meeow |
| §;^() | the law is an ass |
| :^) | if you ain't pretty you'd better be nice |
| :-l | so? |
| :-z | yeah I'm cross |
| (:-& | angry |
| >< | absolutely livid |

| | |
|---|---|
| ~ :-( | steaming mad |
| ( :+( | ooh I'm scared |
| };-> | you are a rude devil |
| :-* | bitter, moi? |
| :-6 | sour, sure |
| :-J | tongue-in-cheek |
| :-C | I don't believe it! |
| I:-I | stubborn |
| :-] | obnoxious |

| | |
|---|---|
| **<=8:-)** | you are a dickhead |
| **=:-)** | lose the moustache lady |
| **:-)}** | … and the goatee |
| **r:-)** | mmm, ponytail spells loser |
| **?:)** | one hair combed over makes no difference, you are still bald |
| **(:-)** | shame you lost the last hair |
| **:-)K-** | a shirt and tie at the gym – please? |

| | |
|---|---|
| **:)))** | hugging that beer belly is like waking up holding a cold hot-water bottle |
| **:-£** | I wouldn't say you were mean, but you would rather swallow your cash than spend it |
| **:^U** | forget it |
| **O-S-<** | I'm outta here |
| **TEXT** | YELLING |

[ : — (

# ActYaAgeNt
# YaShuSIz

**Act your age, not your shoe size**

**DoUEvnNoWotThtMEns?**
> do you even know what that means?

**IflAmWotRU?**  If I am, what are you?

**INoUR**  I know you are

**INoUR1**  I know you are one

**IsThtTBstUCanDo?**
is that the best you
can do?

**MAkMe!** make me!

**SAm2U** same to you

**SAm2Uw/NobzOn**
same to you with
knobs on

**ShtUp** shut up

**YoMoMa!** so's your mother!

# GeTNDwn2BiZnZ

**Hard core insults**

**ALMth&Trsrs**  all mouth and trousers

**ALP$&Wnd**  all piss and wind

**Anrk**  anorak

**A$HOl**  asshole

**A$Kkr**  ass kicker

**A$Lkr**  ass licker

**A$W**  asswipe

| | |
|---|---|
| **Arhed** | airhead |
| **ArmCndE** | arm candy |
| **BEst** | beast |
| **BGr** | bagger |
| **BildrsBm** | builders bum |
| **BMBO** | bimbo |
| **BmClEvj** | bum cleavage |
| **BnanaNOs** | banana nose |
| **BOb** | boob |

| | |
|---|---|
| **BOB** | booby |
| **BOnhed** | bonehead |
| **Borin** | boring |
| **BOzBLE** | booze belly |
| **BOZO** | bozo |
| **BrLOhed** | brillohead |
| **BtmFEdr** | bottom feeder |
| **BTr1/2** | bitter half (husband, wife, partner) |
| **BuThed** | butthead |

| | |
|---|---|
| **CS** | chicken sh*t |
| **DB** | dirtbag |
| **Dgbrth** | dogbreath |
| **DH** | dickhead |
| **DiVE** | divvy |
| **DngBt** | dingbat |
| **DpStk** | dipstick |
| **Drk** | dork |
| **DrkbrAN** | dorkbrain |

| | |
|---|---|
| **DrmaQEn** | drama queen |
| **DrOg** | droog (sidekick) |
| **DuL** | dull |
| **DwEb** | dweeb |
| **Ejit** | eejit (idiot) |
| **FEnd** | fiend |
| **FF** | fart-face |
| **404 FNF** | file not found |
| **FngusFAC** | fungus-face |

| | |
|---|---|
| **Gbln** | goblin |
| **Grmbo** | grimbo |
| **GrO$** | gross |
| **K** | knob |
| **Ken** | trendy plastic-looking boy (e.g. Barbie's boyfriend) |
| **KltZ** | klutz |
| **LAmO** | lamo |
| **LardBckt** | lard bucket |

| | |
|---|---|
| **Lmp** | lump |
| **LOnETUn** | looney-tune |
| **MGt** | maggot |
| **MLLthed** | mullethead |
| **MNchkn** | munchkin (short) |
| **MnDNmn** | mind-numbing |
| **MngBg** | minge-bag (miser) |
| **Mnsta** | monster |
| **Mong** | mongrel |

| | |
|---|---|
| **MowsbrAn** | mousebrain |
| **Nmwd** | nimwad |
| **Nome** | gnome |
| **Nrd** | nerd |
| **OFnsve** | offensive |
| **Ogr** | ogre |
| **PEBrAn** | peabrain |
| **PgDg** | pig dog |
| **Pklp$** | picklepuss |

| **Plnkr** | plonker |
| **PrkFAc** | prick-face |
| **Prwn** | prawn |
| **PZaFAc** | pizza-face |
| **RB** | ratbag |
| **RePTL** | reptile |
| **Rpulsve** | repulsive |
| **SA** | social airhead |
| **SaDO** | saddo |
| **Sadsak** | sadsack |

| **SchmO** | schmo |
| **ScmBg** | scumbag |
| **ScZBg** | scuzzbag |
| **ScZBL** | scuzzball |
| **Shrta$** | shortass |
| **SkrwbL** | screwball |
| **SmLeSox** | smelly socks |
| **Stnkpot** | stinkpot |
| **StNNdMLLt** | stunned mullet |

| | |
|---|---|
| **StUpd** | stupid |
| **Swmpbrth** | swampbreath |
| **Tbg** | teabag |
| **TOL** | tub of lard |
| **TOrg** | toerag |
| **TrLL** | troll |
| **Trndoid** | trendoid (trendy but robotic) |
| **2wcr** | twicer |
| **UglE** | ugly |

| | |
|---|---|
| **WakO** | whacko |
| **Wmp** | wimp |
| **Wrf** | worf |
| **Yak** | yak |
| **YdLOd** | wide load |
| **YOyO** | yoyo |
| **YPPuP** | yuppie puppy<br>(new rich kid) |
| **Zt** | zit (spot) |
| **ZTFAc** | zitface |

# DntBCrOL

**Don't be cruel – when good love turns bad**

**AGoNaBmpNoMorW/NoBgFatWmn**
      ain't gonna bump no more with no big fat woman

**ALOvaNow**    all over now

**BABIDntCAr**    baby I don't care

**BeTaLuvNxtTIm**
      better love next time

**BlaBlaBla**    blah, blah, blah

| | |
|---|---|
| **BrnBABBrn** | burn, baby, burn |
| **CrEp** | creep |
| **CrOl2BKInd** | cruel to be kind |
| **Crwl** | crawl |
| **DrGnMeDwn** | dragging me down |
| **DvllnDsGls** | devil in disguise |
| **Dvors** | divorce |
| **EtTRch** | eat the rich |
| **EtYa<3Out** | eat your heart out |

| | |
|---|---|
| **EtYasIfHOI** | eat yourself whole |
| **EvlWmn** | evil woman |
| **EvreBoDsL@U** | everybody's laughing at you |
| **FOInYasIf** | fooling yourself |
| **GEkStnkBrth** | geek stink breath |
| **GetALIf** | get a life |
| **GOAwALtleGrl** | go away little girl |

**GOBak2YaPlnt**
go back to your planet

**ICntStndUBAB**
I can't stand you baby

**ImGoNaGtUSuka**
I'm gonna get you sucker

**RUReD2B<3Brkn?**
are you ready to be heartbroken?

**TBtchIsBak**
the bitch is back

**2Mch2Ltle2LAt**

        too much, too little,
        too late

**URAnACdntWAtn2HPn**

        you are an accident
        waiting to happen

**YaBumLOksBigInTht**

        your bum looks big in that

# MdgtInslts
**No noses – no more Mr Nice Guy**

| | |
|---|---|
| :} | er? |
| :> | der? |
| :@ | what? |
| :D | yeah, I'm laughing at you |
| :) :) :) | loud guffaw |
| :I | hmmm... |
| ;) | smirking |

| | |
|---|---|
| :[ | real downer |
| :O | yelling |
| :V | shouting |
| :C | liar |
| :/) | not funny |
| ;? | wry remark, tongue in cheek |
| ;} | leer |
| : t | pouting |

| | |
|---|---|
| ll | of course you are not boring (asleep) |
| ^o | snoring |
| :k | biting my lip |
| :] | sarcasm is the lowest form of wit |
| '! | grim |
| ''' | sour puss |
| 'P | (profile) sticking tongue out |

| | |
|---|---|
| **'T** | keeping a straight face (profile) |
| **'U** | yawning (profile) |
| **'V** | shouting (profile) |
| **'Y**<br>**'** | whistling (profile) |
| **\\** | frowning (profile) |
| **'v** | talking (profile) |
| **__!** | that's enough |
| **:!** | foot in mouth |
| **8O** | omigod! |

| | |
|---|---|
| :@ | it's true, I swear |
| X-( | you are mad |
| >:-< | sure I'm mad |
| :(*) | you make me sick |
| :-S | make sense |
| lP | yuk |
| :-8( | condescending stare |
| M-),:X),:-M | oh sure, sees no evil, hears no evil, speaks no evil |

| | |
|---|---|
| 8-S | sees all evil |
| o= | a burning candle for flames (shouting messages of an unpleasant nature) |
| i-=<***i | CAUTION: has flame thrower |
| i-=<*** __. | CAUTION: has flame thrower and uses it! |
| i-=<****** o-(==< | CAUTION: has flame thrower and uses it! |

`-=`  a doused candle to end a flame

`:——————)`  you are a big liar

# UNoWotUCnDo
**You know what you can do**


**ByMEtsGrlSOWot?**

        boy meets girl, so what?

**GOPlAlnTraFk**

        go play in traffic

**IfUHdABrAnUdBDAnjrus**

        if you had a brain you
        would be dangerous

**IfUWnt2AMndREdr**
**TherWldBNoChrge**

> if you went to a mind
> reader there would be
> no charge

**INoWenURLlinYaLpsMov**

> I know when you are
> lying, your lips move

**LItsOnDorOpnNo1In**

> lights on, door open,
> no one in

**TLItsROnBtNo1IsHOm**

> the lights are on but
> no one is home

**TWhElsMvnBtTHmstrsDEd**

> the wheel's moving but
> the hamster's dead

**UDntNoTMninOfTWrdFear**
**InFctUDntNoTMninOfALotOfWrds**

> you don't know the
> meaning of the word fear.
> In fact you don't know
> the meaning of a lot of
> words

**URAsMchUsAsMdGrdsOnATortus**

> you are as much use as
> mudguards on a tortoise

**URAsUsfLAsAChocl8Tpot**

you are as useful as a chocolate teapot

**URLIkTVnusDMIIoVBtifl BtNotALTher**

you are like the Venus de Milo – very beautiful but not all there

**UR1SndwchShrtOfAPiKnk**

you are one sandwich short of a picnic

**UvGotAsMchClaSAsTrnWLPApr**

you've got as much class as torn wallpaper

**WenILOkIntoYaiisIcnCNo1isDrIvn**

> when I look into your eye
> I can see no one is
> driving

**:-(YaBrAnIsntABgAsYa(_,,_)**

> what a pity your brain
> isn't as big
> as your bottom

**YaLiftDsntREchTTopFlOr**

> your lift doesn't reach
> the top floor

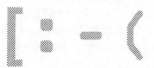

# ImLOkin@ U&IDntLIkWotIC

**I'm looking at you and I don't like what I see**

## AtLEstIDntHavAFAcLIkABmusdHaDck

at least I don't have a face like a bemused haddock

## IBetUCntSwm UCIdntKEpYaMthSht4LngEnuf

I bet you can't swim, you couldn't keep your mouth shut for long enough

**IfYaMthWozNEBiGrUWdntHav NEFAcLft2Wsh**

> if your mouth was any bigger you wouldn't have any face left to wash

**IvSEnAHeltheaLOkinFAcOnAPIrtFlag**

> I've seen a healthier looking face on a pirate flag

**IvSEnBeTaBoDsInACarBrkrsYrd**

> I've seen better bodies in a car breaker's yard

**IvSEnMreHarOnABlyudBL**

> I've seen more hair on a billiard ball

**RThOsFEtYaOwnOrRUBrkn**
**ThmIn4ADuk?**

> are those feet your own
> or are you breaking them
> in for a duck

**TLstTImISawLegsLIk**
**ThtTherWozAMSgeTId21OfThm**

> the last time I saw legs
> like that there was a
> message tied to one of
> them

**TSIzURIBetUHavYaOwnPstCOd**

> the size you are, I bet
> you have your own
> post-code

**UCldGetAJobAsADcoy4AWAlinShp**

you could get a job
as a decoy for a
whaling ship

**UCldSwatFllsW/thseErs**

you could swat flies
with those ears

**ULOkLlk$1MALGrEn&RinklE**

you look like a million
dollars – all green
and wrinkly

**URSoMEnTQunBlnks**
**WenUOpnYaWaLT**

> you are so mean the
> queen blinks when you
> open your wallet

**URSOOldUCnRmbaWen**
**MObDikWozOnlyATdPOl**

> you are so old you
> can remember when
> Moby Dick was only a
> tadpole

**URSOOldUCnRmbaWen**
**TDedCWasJstIL**

> you are so old you can
> remember when the
> Dead Sea was just ill

**URSOOldUCnRmbaWenMdmeBuTrFly
WasOnlyACatrpLa**

you are so old you can
remember when
Madame Butterfly was
only a caterpillar

**URSOShrtIfUPuLdUpYrSoxUdBBlndfld**

you are so short that if
you pulled up your socks
you would be blindfold

**UvGotAFAcLlkASqEzdTBag**

you've got a face like a
squeezed tea-bag

**UvGotANIcPrOfLgsSpecIlyTLft1**

you have got a nice pair of legs, especially the left one

**UvGotMreChnsThnAChInEsFOnBOk**

you've got more chins than a Chinese phone book

**YaFEtRSoBigUCldStmpOutBushFIrs**

your feet are so big you could stamp out forest fires

**YaiisRLIkPOIsMuDyPOIs**

your eyes are like pools – muddy pools

**YaMemresSoBadYaMama**
**Used2rapYaLnchInARdMap**

> your memory's so bad
> your mother used to
> wrap your lunch in
> a road map

**YaTEthRLIkT\*\*sThyCumOut@Nite**

> your teeth are like the
> stars – they come out at
> night

# Bak2YaR0ts
**Basic abbreviations & acronyms
for fast talkers**

| | |
|---|---|
| **AAM** | as a matter of fact |
| **AB** | ah bless! |
| **AFAIC** | as far as I'm concerned |
| **AFAIK** | as far as I know |
| **AKA** | also known as |
| **ASAP** | as soon as possible |

| | |
|---|---|
| **ATB** | all the best |
| **B** | be |
| **BBFN** | bye bye for now |
| **BBL** | be back later |
| **BCNU** | be seeing you |
| **B4** | before |
| **BFN** | bye for now |
| **BRB** | be right back |
| **BTW** | by the way |

| | |
|---|---|
| **BUKT** | but you knew that |
| **Bwd** | backward |
| **C** | see |
| **CHYA!** | chill ya! |
| **CMIIW** | correct me if I'm wrong |
| **CU** | see you |
| **CYA** | see you |
| **Doin** | doing |
| **DOA** | drunk on arrival |

| | |
|---|---|
| **d8** | date |
| **EOL** | end of lecture |
| **FAQ** | frequently asked question(s) |
| **FITB** | fill in the blank |
| **F2T** | free to talk |
| **Fwd** | forward |
| **FWIW** | for what it's worth |
| **FYI** | for your information |
| **GB** | God bless |

| | |
|---|---|
| **G2G** | got to go |
| **GD&R** | grinning, ducking and running (after snide remark) |
| **GG** | good game |
| **Gr8** | great |
| **Gonna** | going to |
| **HAND** | have a nice day |
| **HTH** | hope this/to help(s) |
| **IAC** | in any case |

| **IAE** | in any event |
| **IANAL** | I am not a lawyer (but...) |
| **ICCL** | I couldn't care less |
| **ICL** | in Christian love |
| **IDK** | I don't know |
| **IIRC** | if I recall correctly |
| **IMOTT** | I'm on the train |
| **IMCO** | in my considered opinion |
| **IMHO** | in my humble opinion |

| **IMNSHO** | in my not so humble opinion |
| **IMO** | in my opinion |
| **IOOH** | I'm out of here |
| **IOW** | in other words |
| **IRSYHAFS** | I remain, sir, your humble and faithful servant |
| **IU2U** | it's up to you |
| **IUDKIDKWD** | if you don't know I don't know who does |

| | |
|---|---|
| **IUKWIM** | if you know what I mean |
| **IUKWIMAITYD** | |
| | if you know what I mean and I think you do |
| **IYSS** | if you say so |
| **JM2p** | just my 2 pennyworth |
| **KIT** | keep in touch |
| **LKIT** | like it |
| **L8** | late |
| **L8r** | later |

| **Luv** | love |
| **LOL** | lots of luck or laughing out loud |
| **M4I** | mad for it |
| **MGB** | may God bless |
| **MHOTY** | my hat's off to you |
| **Mob** | mobile |
| **Msg** | message |
| **NE** | any |
| **NE1** | anyone |

| | |
|---|---|
| **NEPlAc** | any place |
| **NETlm** | anytime |
| **NEwer** | any where |
| **NH** | nice hand |
| **N1!** | nice one! |
| **NO1** | no one |
| **NRN** | no reply necessary |
| **NT2NITE** | not tonight |
| **OIC** | oh, I see |

| | |
|---|---|
| **ON4** | on for |
| **OTOH** | on the other hand |
| **PAW** | parents are watching |
| **PCM** | please call me |
| **PLS** | please |
| **PPL** | people |
| **PS** | post script |
| **R** | are |
| **ROF** | rolling on the floor |

| | |
|---|---|
| **ROFL** | rolling on the floor laughing |
| **RU** | are you? |
| **RUOK?** | are you OK? |
| **RUUP4IT?** | are you up for it? |
| **SIT** | stay in touch |
| **SITD** | still in the dark |
| **Sk8** | skate |
| **Sk8r** | skater |
| **SMS** | short message service |

| | |
|---|---|
| **S2US** | speak to you soon |
| **StrA** | stray |
| **Str8** | straight |
| **ST2MORO?** | same time tomorrow? |
| **SUM1** | someone |
| **SWG** | scientific wild guess |
| **SWALK** | sent with a loving kiss |
| **T** | the |
| **THNQ** | thank you |

| | |
|---|---|
| **Thx** | thanks |
| **TIA** | thanks in advance |
| **TIFN** | that's it for now |
| **Ti2GO** | time to go |
| **TPTB** | the powers that be |
| **TTFN** | ta ta for now |
| **TTUL** | talk to you later |
| **TUVM** | thank you very much |
| **TWIMC** | to whom it may concern |

| | |
|---|---|
| **U** | you |
| **UR** | you are |
| **U4IT** | up for it |
| **WAN2** | want to |
| **WAN2TLK?** | want to talk? |
| **WA$U?** | what's up? |
| **W/** | with |
| **W\** | without |
| **Wknd** | weekend |

| | |
|---|---|
| **WRT** | with respect to |
| **WTTW** | word to the wise |
| **YA** | your |
| **YKWYCD** | you know what you can do |
| **YMMV** | your mileage may vary (you may not have the same luck I did) |
| **YWIA** | you're welcome in advance |

| | |
|---|---|
| **1** | one |
| **2** | to, too |
| **2day** | today |
| **2moro** | tomorrow |
| **2nite** | tonight |
| **3sum** | threesome |
| **4** | for |
| **<G>** | grinning |
| **<J>** | joking |

| | |
|---|---|
| **<L>** | laughing |
| **<O>** | shouting |
| **<S>** | smiling |
| **<Y>** | yawning |
| **$** | double S |
| **%** | double B |

# TeLItHowItIs
**Basic emoticons**

| | |
|---|---|
| :-) | happy |
| :-( | sad |
| I-) | hee hee |
| I-D | ho ho |
| :-> | hey hey |
| :-( | boo hoo |

| | |
|---|---|
| :-I | hmmm |
| :-O | oops |
| :-* | ooops |
| :-o | uh oh! |
| I:-O | no explanation given |
| :-o | oh, no! |
| #:-o | oh, no! |
| <:-O | eeek! |
| O:-) | for those innocent souls |

| | |
|---|---|
| **:-)))** | reeeaaaalllly happy |
| **;-) or P-)** | wink, wink, nudge, nudge |
| **:-7** | that was a wry remark |
| **:-)~** | I am drooling (in anticipation) |
| **:-9** | I am licking my lips |
| **(-:** | I am left-handed |
| **:'-(** | I am crying |
| **:'-)** | I am so happy, I am crying |

| | |
|---|---|
| :~( | I am bawling |
| :-@ | I am screaming |
| :-& | I feel tongue-tied |
| <&-I | I feel foolish and tearful |
| :-S | my last message didn't make sense |
| :^Y | I turn my poker face away |
| :-X | my lips are sealed |
| :-# | my lips are still sealed |

| | |
|---|---|
| **:-/** | I am sceptical |
| **:-T** | I am keeping a straight face |
| **o'!** | I am feeling pretty grim (profile) |
| **o'"'** | I am pursing my lips (profile) |
| **o'J** | smiling (profile) |
| **o'T** | keeping a straight face (profile) |
| **o'U** | yawning (profile) |

| | |
|---|---|
| **o'V** | shouting (profile) |
| **o'Y** | whistling (profile) |
| **o'\** | frowning (profile) |
| **o'v** | talking (profile) |
| **o'w** | lying (profile) |
| **7=^>** | I am happy (3/4 view) |
| **:-S** | I am confused |
| **:*(** | I am crying softly |
| **:-@!** | I am cursing |

| | |
|---|---|
| -" | whistling casually |
| :-e | I am disappointed |
| (:-... | I am heartbroken |
| I-I | I am going to sleep |
| :*) | I am drunk |
| %-) | I am drunk but happy |
| *L* | I am blotto (sideways) |
| :*)? | are you drunk? |
| :#) | I am drunk every night |

| | |
|---|---|
| %*@:-( | I am hungover with a headache |
| :^) | I have personality |
| d :-) | hats off to your great idea |
| :-(*) | that comment made me sick |
| (@ @) | you're kidding! |
| (:-IK- | this is a formal message |
| (-_-) | this is my secret smile (sideways) |
| **-( | I am very, very shocked |

| | |
|---|---|
| :^D | great! I like it! |
| M:-) | respect |
| :-$ | put your money where your mouth is |
| >-COD | I am "floundering" for something to say |
| /O\ | I am ducking |
| .^, | I am looking sideways/happy |
| =-o | I am surprised |
| <=-O | I am frightened |

| | |
|---|---|
| =-◇ | I am awestruck |
| (]:-) | I am gung ho |
| :~(~~~ | I am moved to tears |
| O-(==< | I am chastised and/or chagrined |
| __. | I am properly chastised and/or chagrined |
| __/~`-'~\_/ | I don't follow your line of thought |
| I-{ | "Good Grief!" (Charlie Brown?) |

**===:[OO']>:===**    I have been railroaded

**=^)**    I am open-minded

**\o/**    PTL (praise the lord, or pass the loot?) (sideways)

**OO**    please read now (headlights on msg)

[:-(

*Now you can order other little books directly from
Michael O'Mara Books.
All at £1.99 each including postage (UK only)*

*The Little Book of Farting -*        ISBN 1-85479-445-0
*The Little Book of Stupid Men -*     ISBN 1-85479-454-X
*The Little Toilet Book -*            ISBN 1-85479-456-6
*The Little Book of Venom -*          ISBN 1-85479-446-9
*The Little Book of Pants -*          ISBN 1-85479-477-9
*The Little Book of Pants 2 -*        ISBN 1-85479-557-0
*The Little Book of Bums -*           ISBN 1-85479-561-9
*The Little Book of Revenge -*        ISBN 1-85479-562-7
*The Little Book of Voodoo -*         ISBN 1-85479-560-0
*The Little Book of Blondes -*        ISBN 1-85479-558-9
*The Little Book of Magical Love Spells -*
                                      ISBN 1-85479-559-7
*WAN2TLK? ltle bk of txt msgs -*      ISBN 1-85479-678-X
*LUVTLK? ltle bk of luv txt -*        ISBN 1-85479-890-1
*RUUP4IT? ltle bk of txt d8s -*       ISBN 1-85479-892-8
*The Little Book of Cockney Rhyming Slang -*
                                      ISBN 1-85479-825-1
*The Little Book of Gay Gags -*       ISBN 1-85479-590-2

*The Little Book of Irish Grannies' Remedies -*
ISBN 1-85479-828-6
*The Little Book of Scottish Grannies' Remedies -*
ISBN 1-85479-829-4
*The Little Book of Irish Wit & Wisdom -*
ISBN 1-85479-827-8
*The Little Book of Scottish Wit & Wisdom -*
ISBN 1-85479-826-X

*Postage and packing outside the UK:*
*Europe: add 20% of retail price*
*Rest of the world: add 30% of retail price*

To order any Michael O'Mara book please call our
credit-card hotline:
020 8324 5652

Michael O'Mara Bookshop
BVCD
32-34 Park Royal Road
London NW10 7LN